BRIGHT
IDEA
BOOKS

HOW DO
Spiders
HEAR?

Nancy Furstinger

raintree

a Capstone company — publishers for children

Raintree is an imprint of Capstone Global Library Limited, a company incorporated in England and Wales having its registered office at 264 Banbury Road, Oxford, OX2 7DY – Registered company number: 6695582

www.raintree.co.uk
myorders@raintree.co.uk

Text © Capstone Global Library Limited 2019
The moral rights of the proprietor have been asserted.

Edited by Maddie Spalding
Designed by Becky Daum
Production by Colleen McLaren
Printed and bound in India

ISBN 978 1 4747 7512 0
22 21 20 19 18
10 9 8 7 6 5 4 3 2 1

British Library Cataloguing in Publication Data
A full catalogue record for this book is available from the British Library.

Acknowledgements
iStockphoto: jerbarber, 6–7, Joe_Guetzloff, 24–25, KirsanovV, 25; Newscom: H. Bellmann/
picture alliance/blickwinkel/H, 19, Mark Moffett/Minden Pictures, 26–27; Shutterstock
Images: Aleks Melnik, cover (music notes), Alen thien, 9, 28, Cathy Keifer, 5, 20–21, 30–31,
davemhuntphotography, 10–11, dmvphotos, 23, Dr Morley Read, 14–15, 16–17, Krom1975, cover
(spider), MF Photo, 12–13
Design Elements: iStockphoto, Red Line Editorial, and Shutterstock Images

We would like to thank Michael L. Draney, PhD, from the Department of Natural and Applied
Sciences, University of Wisconsin-Green Bay for his invaluable help in the preparation of
this book.

CONTENTS

CHAPTER 1

TRAPPED!

A spider waits. It sits at the edge of its web. A fly buzzes nearby. It doesn't see the web. It zooms into the trap. The web is made of silk. The silk is sticky. The fly can't escape.

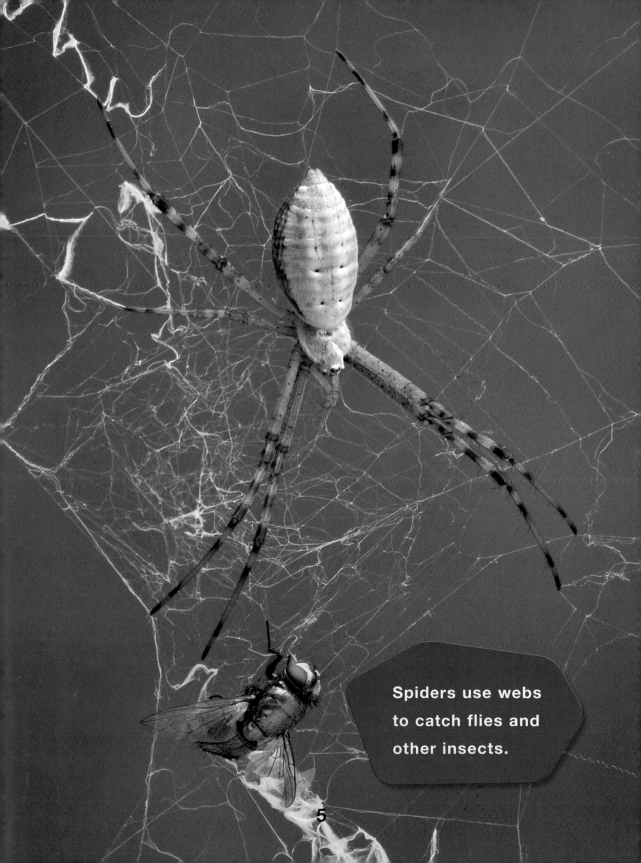

Spiders use webs to catch flies and other insects.

5

A spider rolls its prey in silk to make sure it cannot escape.

6

The spider doesn't have ears. It has eyes. Its eyes cannot see well. But the spider can still sense the fly's movement. The spider moves quickly to its **prey**. It sinks its **fangs** into the fly. The fangs deliver **venom**. Now the fly cannot move. The spider wraps the fly in silk. It will save this meal for later.

CHAPTER 2

HEARING
with Hairs

Scientists once thought spiders were deaf. Then scientists discovered something amazing. Spiders don't need ears. They have other ways of sensing sounds.

Scientists have studied spiders, such as the jumping spider, to discover how they sense sounds.

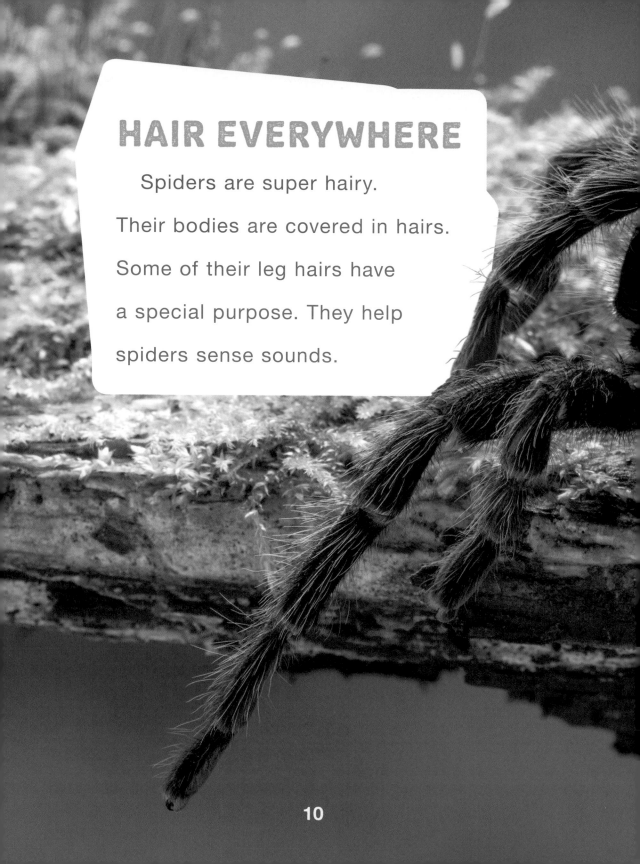

HAIR EVERYWHERE

Spiders are super hairy. Their bodies are covered in hairs. Some of their leg hairs have a special purpose. They help spiders sense sounds.

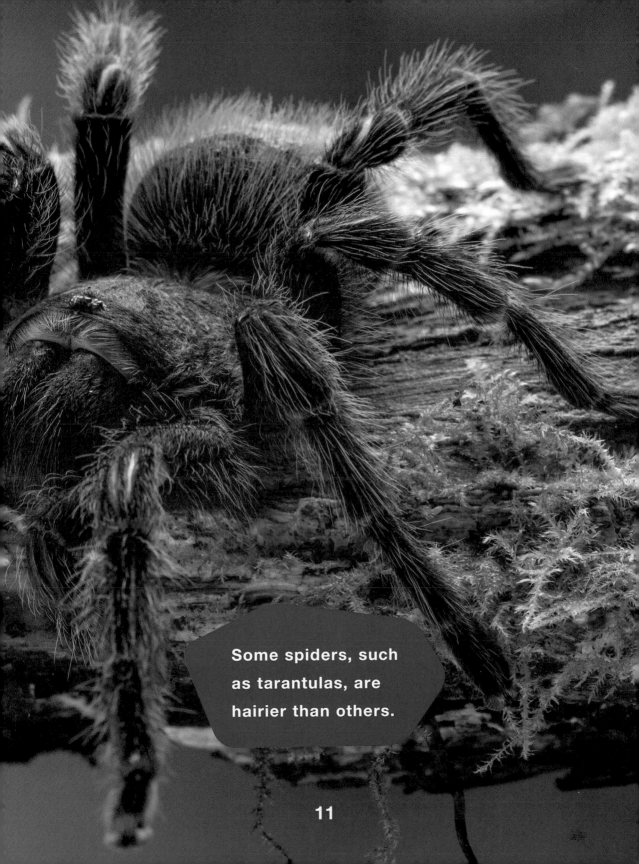

Some spiders, such as tarantulas, are hairier than others.

11

Sound travels when air moves back and forth. These movements are **sound waves**. Humans have ears. Inside each ear is an eardrum. The eardrum is a **membrane**. Sound reaches the eardrum. The eardrum **vibrates**. Other parts of the ear vibrate too. This includes tiny bones in the ear. The movement carries a message to the brain. The brain works out what the sound is.

Spiders sense sounds differently. Sound waves wiggle special hairs on a spider's legs. The spider feels the movement.

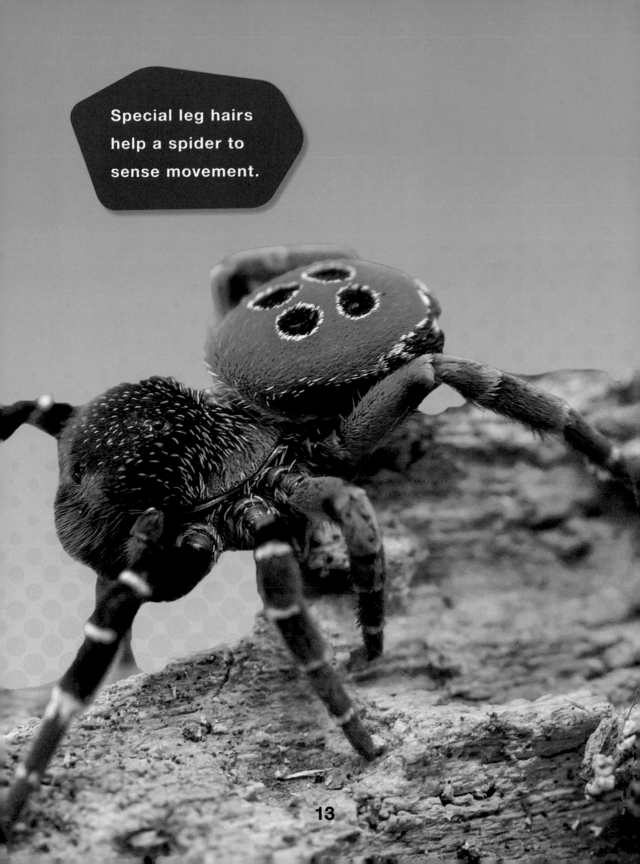

Special leg hairs help a spider to sense movement.

A spider's hairs help it sense **predators**. Wasps hunt spiders. Animals such as lizards also eat spiders. Each predator moves in a different way. Each predator makes different sound waves. This helps spiders tell the difference between predators and prey.

SPECIAL ORGANS

Spiders have special **organs** on their legs. A spider has an outer shell. This is a skeleton on the outside of the spider's body. It is called an **exoskeleton**. The special organs are on this shell. They are made up of tiny slits. Each slit is a different length. The slits look like harp strings. Vibrations cause the slits to change shape. This helps the spider sense movement.

slits

slit organ

A spider's leg organs are made up of many tiny slits.

EXOSKELETONS

A spider is born with an exoskeleton. It sheds this shell as it grows. A new shell grows in the old one's place.

CHAPTER 3

FINDING a Mate

The slits on a spider's legs help it to find a **mate**. Some male spiders scratch leaves. They do this with their mouths. Some also drum on leaves.

They use their **abdomens** to do this.

Female spiders feel the movements.

The slits on their legs change shape.

This lets them know a mate is on

the plant.

Some spiders find mating partners by scratching on leaves.

PURRING SPIDERS

Some male wolf spiders purr to find mates. The spider finds a dead leaf. It taps the leaf with its body. This makes the leaf vibrate. The leaf acts like a phone line. Sound waves travel through it.

WOLF SPIDERS

A wolf spider's purrs are so loud that humans can hear them.

**Dead and dry leaves
carry sound further than
leaves that are not dry.**

The waves hit leaves near a female
spider. The slits on the female's legs
change shape. The female knows a mate
is near.

CHAPTER 4

MUSICAL
Spiders

A spider makes silk in its body. It pushes out silk through an organ in its abdomen. Silk is strong. It is also flexible. It can stretch without breaking. Prey gets caught in the silk. But the web doesn't break.

Spiders use their webs to catch prey. They also use their webs to communicate. They pluck the silk like a guitar. The strands vibrate.

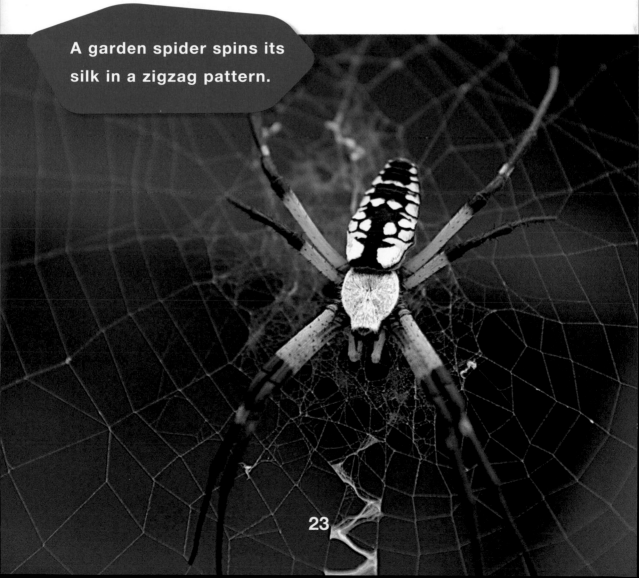

A garden spider spins its silk in a zigzag pattern.

Spiders can make webs in different shapes. The Pennsylvania grass spider's web is shaped like a funnel.

Male spiders pluck the webs of female spiders. This vibrates the strands. The female senses the movement. The male plucks the strands in a certain way. This tells the female there is a mate on her web.

STRONG WEBS

A spider's web needs to stay strong. Strong webs stop prey from escaping. Spiders pluck at the strands. Then they listen to the echoes. They may find weak spots. Then they remake their webs.

A female spider (left) and a male spider (right) meet to mate.

PREY OR PREDATOR?

Some jumping spiders hunt other spiders. The jumping spider plucks the other spider's web. It plucks wildly. The other spider thinks prey is caught in its web. It goes towards the movement. The jumping spider catches and eats it! A spider's senses are powerful. But they don't always help it survive!

A jumping spider (left) catches larger spiders by pretending to be prey.

SPIDER SILK

Some spider silk is stronger than steel.

GLOSSARY

abdomen
the back part of a spider's body

exoskeleton
a hard outer shell on animals such as insects and spiders

fang
a needle-like mouthpart that injects venom into prey

mate
a partner that an animal makes babies with

membrane
a thin layer of tissue that covers part of the body

organ
a part of an animal's body that has a special job

predator
an animal that hunts and eats other animals

prey
an animal that is hunted by other animals

sound wave
a wave formed when a sound is made

venom
a poison that is produced by an animal to defend itself and kill prey

vibrate
to move back and forth

TOP FIVE REASONS WHY
SPIDERS
ARE AWESOME

1. They use special organs and the hair on their legs to sense movements.

2. Their skeletons are on the outside of their bodies.

3. Their hearts pump blue blood.

4. Some spiders can catch bats in giant webs.

5. Some spiders spin webs while they are under water. They use these webs to breathe.

ACTIVITY

Spiders do not sense sound waves in the same way that humans do. Try out this experiment to discover how spiders sense sounds:

WHAT YOU WILL NEED

water

orange juice

vegetable oil

3 glasses

1 spoon

INSTRUCTIONS

1. Fill each glass with a different type of liquid. Put the same amount of liquid in each glass.

2. Hit each glass with the spoon. The liquid inside the glass will vibrate. This creates a sound. We hear these sound waves with our ears. But spiders would sense them with their legs and hairs.

3. Next, try using different amounts of liquid in each glass. Hit the glasses with the spoon. How does the amount and type of liquid affect the sound? How might this be similar to how spiders tell prey from predators?

FIND OUT MORE

Ready to discover more fun facts about spiders?
Learn more with these resources.

Books

Insects and Spiders (DK, 2019)

Spiders, Laura Marsh (National Geographic, 2011)

Super Spiders, Charlotte Guillain (Raintree, 2013)

Websites

National Geographic: Black Widow
kids.nationalgeographic.com/animals/black-widow/
    #black-widow-sideways-web.jpg

Smithsonian Education: Under the Spell of Spiders
www.smithsonianeducation.org/educators/lesson_plans/under_spell_spiders
    spiderspecifics.html

INDEX